Elegies & Vacations

Elegies & Vacations, Hank Lazer's eleventh book of poetry, is Lazer's fourth large collection of poetry, following *Days* (Lavender Ink, 2002), *3 of 10* (Chax Press, 1996), and *Doublespace: Poems 1971–1989* (Segue, 1992). A noted critic, Lazer's two-volume *Opposing Poetries* (Northwestern University Press) appeared in 1996. With Charles Bernstein, Lazer edits the Modern and Contemporary Poetics Series for the University of Alabama, where Lazer is Assistant Vice President and Professor of English.

Elegies & Vacations

Hank Lazer

SALT

PUBLISHED BY SALT PUBLISHING
PO Box 937, Great Wilbraham, Cambridge PDO CB1 5JX United Kingdom
PO Box 202, Applecross, Western Australia 6153

© Hank Lazer, 2004

The right of Hank Lazer to be identified as the
author of this work has been asserted by him in accordance
with Section 77 of the Copyright, Designs and Patents Act 1988.

First published 2004

Printed and bound in the United Kingdom by Lightning Source

Typeset in Swift 9.5 / 13

ISBN 1 84471 008 4 paperback

SP

1 3 5 7 9 8 6 4 2

To Jake Berry, Jon Berry, and Wayne Sides

Contents

Acknowledgments

Several of these poems first appeared in *Hambone* (Santa Cruz – Nathaniel Mackey), *Chicago Review* (Chicago – Devin Johnston), *Boxkite* (Sydney, Australia – James Taylor), *XCP: Cross-Cultural Poetics* (Minneapolis – Mark Nowak), *muse apprentice guild* (San Diego – Augie Highland), *New Orleans Review* (Bill Lavender), and *Tinfish* (Honolulu – Susan Schultz). Thanks to the editors.

This One will be published as a chapbook by Quarry Press (Shippensburg, Pennsylvania: 2004). My thanks to Andrew Mossin for the chapbook and for permission to reprint.

Deathwatch for My Father was published as a chapbook by Chax Press (Tucson : 2003). My thanks to Charles Alexander for the chapbook and for permission to reprint.

Several of these poems appear in *As It Is*, a chapbook published by Diaeresis Chapbooks (Boca Raton : 1999). My thanks to the publishers, Mark Scroggins and Bill Burmeister, for the chapbook and for permission to reprint.

Cover photo by Wayne Sides – "The Prophet" – Birmingham, Alabama (1977). Reprinted with permission of the photographer.

"to what are we ancestral"

do they speak within me

now that they are dead

they *were* here   what *are*

they to me   & what *were* they

couldn't they have been

nearly anyone telling those

stories   they made

a claim on me   i carried

forward their stories   i pledged

to do so   & so

took up this calling of words

i did it with their ear

nonnative to this language

& i unaccustomed to

this genre   & the people of it

Portrait

Who can say what the day may mean in its
parqueted intricacy, its lacquered imperviousness, which, as we know,
    was
built upon a subflooring overly susceptible to dry rot, an
odd name for a fungus brought about by excessive moisture,
which in due course severely cracked and damaged the beams
and joists which were supposed to hold up the whole
goddamned shooting match. The work world proves and reproves
itself inhospitable to language play, a memorandum too strait-laced
    clime
for your slavic improvisation, "The Nude Whirled Sinfully." As for
Suzhou who could say enough about the sycamore-lined streets, the

practical but atouristic canals which so impressed Marco Polo eight
hundred years ago, though now the translations of his travel
writings are keyed to different city names and you cannot
find exactly what he said and prize-winning historians snicker at
Polo's inconsistencies and amusing ethnocentrisms. Sentences stretch
    out this way,
which has become your signatured way, languorous, late nineteenth
    century,
wistful, though a hammock relaxing to the spine and thus
fit habitation for the englobed meat atop said column, rivers
or canals, channels in their own right. For those who
love a complex civic whistling, a tripping hymn in a

minor key, or the few who still sit in the
museum of intensive reading and savor a beautifully phrased cultural
estimation bubbled up as personalized rumination, your loquacious
    threnody proves
to be a sousa music of our time, a wry
march, with a grin, into the sunset of our national
decline. Fuses blow, though exactly what such domestic phenomena
    portend
is anyone's guess. At the dinner table young boys in
their baseball shirts dawdle over vegetables; young girls ponder barbie
accessories. A recent dig demonstrates for certain that the remote
control antedates the development of individual psychology. At some
    point

in the composition, coffee gets replaced as the beverage of
choice by a single malt scotch, and if the reader
is alert and quizzical, her own thoughts will shift into
focus. Once the city was exciting, a place for logarithmic
extraction and pastoral compensation; now, however, we've been
    convinced we're
post- all that. If they would clean up the canals
and paint the stucco homes the mauve the taupe the
tints of rose the tourists love, then Suzhou and its
silk, if the townspeople could take on a hospitable swiss-like
or hawaiian eagerness to please, then fearful busloads of hard

currency would be doled out among rock gardens and rickshaws
bicycling amidst the dolorous sycamores, and you among them with
your boyish grin. It is finally then a comfortable and
even comforting beauty you propose, mostly backward-looking,
         relishing the syrupy
pageant of temporal transformation, its merciful indistinctness, and
         you
the professor of its almost inaudible drip. Eccentric personages
         entertain
us, though the media rein them in, until all become
fully explicable, if not pitiable, within a picture and one
page of simple prose. Which makes me want to say
as my brother-in-law James Odis Parker does, "bite a hog."

Much slips from view, in your hands felt through the
reel, a specific drag to what pulls away, eludes apprehension,
tangible as the soggy tennis ball your dog keeps depositing
in your hand, and equally resistant to absolute articulation except
as your exact description of approximation, which becomes our limited
credo of the knowable, reap as you sew, mixed eloquent
riff attuning to millennium. It's inventory day in the jewelry
store in the mall, and your job, which requires you
to stay after, is to count the cultured pearls and
to categorize their various sheens, which you would never consent

to do if you did not have rent and electricity
bills to pay and an almost desperate need to live
on your own, so you shift from foot to foot
and watch the middle-aged man in the shop across the
way sell rubber-band powered birds that flap and fly in
circles. Even the muzak, trivial and manipulative as it is,
can be savored, *if* one has the leisure and the archness
coincident with a meta-perspective. That is what is meant by
criticism. If the narrative were a little more filled in
you could say whether "twist in the wind" meant an

actual body or a color-changing leaf, though either way it's
metaphorical as all get out. Friends come by to say
they love you, which is nice, but means there must
also be some pressure now to say so. They do
love you, and the best elegy is an early one.
Who would be foolish enough to ask them as we
pass by in our soft-seat compartment and as they go
to the fields at dawn driving the yellow buffalo through
the turgid earth, are you *happy* living this way, only
to encounter an utterly puzzled look, the facial equivalent of

addressee unknown, while we continue to calibrate if not celebrate
the modulations of our daily moods and the larger more
glorious denominations of our individual quotients of personal life
    satisfaction.
Frivolous nationalists, forbidden to read the american cultural
    dipstick, consume
the hourly factoids of how "we" are doing, the electronic
passion play of the well-informed. Open your lunch box and
see what mother packed. What makes the walls sweat, and
shouldn't the return vents be doing a better job? It
gets a little close in here. No matter how far
you wander away you can still hear whispers from the

standard syllabus; as you scribble surreptitiously on the shithouse
    wall,
other words seemingly of equal or greater glory, noble and
memorable sentiments, bleed through, and you are compelled to read
them while you are writing. The four cats with wings—
Harriett, Roger, Thelma, and James—hover over the dumpster, the
child listens to the story mesmerized, in the distance a
new generation is inventing a new version of realism, another
roughening up, which calls quaint the ruminations of a single
voice at dusk and too painterly the cream cheese smear
of purple clouds and too gothic the proleptic thunder clap.

Every Now & Then

5/3/96

is
an admiration of
beauty
what
we seek
take succor
sucker
from this
from that
forensic
melodic
product

≈

the flutter
of
her hand
as her white
suburban
goes by headed
for home

≈

speaking of
contingency
i miss it

& outside of
necessitates

an initial
exhilaration
of thinking

5/4/96

as exactitude
cuts the mat
board hard
frames the de
limited vista
as exactitude
has exactitude
if you will
what is

the flat   the fizz
the carbonation

          of what is

5/19/96

Duncan – *Copy Book entries* – $10
Bernstein – *The Subject* – $6
Loss Glazier – *The Parts* – $5
Joris – *Winnetou* – $5
Ron – Xing – $6
Spahr – *Testimony* – $6

kuszai@acsu.buffalo.edu

5/29/96

first thought
worst thought
quick consecutive
instant invective

this way
we bury
our own
done in

which riches
what done
what wishes
finally for

zip lock
lip synch
dave clark's
trademark rhetoric

which sister
got abused
the brother
busted twice

out of
clay plasma
happens flat
post- pastiche

melopoeia thickens
the plot
upper air
digital flicker

copies distributed
upon request
you presume
diminished communication

sing it
lowdown fell
fret to
bad ladder

for who
it is
beautiful
fortuitous

~

redundant, & he knows it
though to *state* it, on the page, *is*

a particular incarnation of it

the "*no?*" a kind of "*nu?*," yiddish rhetoric

then the stanza that follows, fusing eye &
ear (by means of the ear, by a musical
progression) – by the end an utterly
enigmatic & musically attractive set of
sounds

       p. 137 last stanza (Genesis)
          My poetics ! . . .

goes in next stanza to *inferiority* of current writing,
or at least the equal excellence of prior
soundings

      a beautifully done *page* – p. 138

6/8/96

the

    if this

the pellicle
a particle

set about   exactly as

    has sisters

& none of this

you   if you wish

    i'm not
    i'm not lying

as expressive as

the myth
the breath

    had the celebrant

6/14/96

consecutive

the independent

from the successful

sniffs
hikes
trots on

point at which
the clouds deepen

steeped in transition
which enpurples

the shrub lights come on

the boys continue
to toss the balsa
glider

6/16/96   (father's day)

for sustenance
   today
      first thing

i tasted
   your ashes
      smelled

surprisingly sweet
   what i have
      of them

placed gray pumice
   circling the small
      willow

by your son
   a song with you
      in mind

6/18/96   (plane – Boston to Bangor)

people seem
to me not
very ex
cited by
life   am i
oh
on & off

          ∽

over now
the state
where larry
cooked up his
early work

now gone too
the cramped
his clutching
percussive
witness

          ∽

all elegy
hell
there's nothing
else

～

"the weighted light road   (eigner, *selected poems*, p. 35)

    the dead become eternal"

～

everything sticks
does it
would we
wish it so

best not to
take much
with you

～

cryptic
rock salt

an asterisk

more playful
than mythic

an immediate
pause

≈

arose   some
thing on paper

this prayer
that lyn be well

≈

i know
you
hate the
specific

& now
here you are
stuck in it

≈

an integral
lower limit *flip*
upper limit *grave*

6/19/96   (orono)

ask Mark Scroggins for his DLB
pieces on Zukofsky, Taggart, and Mackey

6/20/96

or   less willed
    registrations

when he went
        back into himself

        he had
            often before

never   except when garrulous
        a verbally
        forthcoming man

                    now that i think of it

            odd
            my father
            chose cremation

6/22/96

held to it

you wouldn't want to be

∾

wit:

you can have it

∾

in habit

on exhibit

rib-it

rib-it

∾

6/22/96   (late evening: for theodore enslin)   *first hearing*

if as you did
ted

as it was
late then

so as you sang
ted

or as you
said then

we were a
wakened

late as it
was then

rose petals were
falling

the precision in
spiring

if as you did
ted

as it was late
then

light as our
breathing

if as you did
ted

on down the way
ted

we heard death was
singing

an air of fathers
an air of the sons

done with sudden
reversals

the singing went on
then

& out of our
hearing

if as you did
ted

not forever not
forever

as it was late
then

& of this sweet
instant

restored to our
living

such as it is
then

6/23/96

is myth

anything other

than resonance

why must it

be given

a proper name

Hank Lazer

For John Cage

we don't go

to find you there

you made it

and you are not there

in its making

you

were not its destination

as the canceled space

in your exact nature

you are there

~

you are there

in your exact nature

as the canceled space

were not its destination

you

in its making

and you are not there

you made it

to find you there

we don't go

Deathwatch for My Father

Charles Lazer September 29, 1926 – February 16, 1996

ever as in
light

12/2/95

one among the many
questions   why am i
writing   in the face of
your dying   (an event
by the way   that has
no face)   one among
your many doctors
says   with regret
yes   it is a matter
of days maybe at most
a few weeks
my mind inclines
to ask   and what
is *it*   perhaps to
turn your death into
linguistic inquiry
a somewhat familiar
terrain   you say
from your hospital bed
"henry   the one thing i
regret about this disease
is that i have it instead
of moamar khadafy"
we *do*   mostly at my
urging   cry together
and say out loud

our love for one another
but mostly your preference
(which i expect as i
get much older
will prove exemplary
though contrary to my
nature) is to talk
lightly   football games
the intricacies of golf
which you still hope
to play
        i went
out this afternoon & played
a few holes hit some
practice shots walked alone
knowing the golf course
is one place i can always
contact you   this day
quite literally wearing one
of your shirts one of your
sweaters playing with
the blade irons you
bought from ben crenshaw
and gave to me
good thing i was alone
because my crying
(to someone else)
would have made no
sense   i began to think
about the last round
we played together
Cypress Point in june
amazingly a crystal clear
warm morning a dream
round at one of the world's

most beautiful courses
a reprieve from your
leukemia   a gift from
a friend   a day to be
savored your way
immersed in our
mostly silent companionship
for the course itself
gave us enough to
think about

as a poet
to think about
that last round
takes me to a rhetorical
hazard   the emotional msg
the flavor enhancing phrases
of the manipulative personal
poem   the vast litany
of "for the last time,"
"finally," "never again,"
"suddenly" "even"
"so much" "ultimately"
"if ever" etcetera
in golf these phrases
amount to hitting the shot
fat   you have been
a major part of my poems
since i wrote "point sur"
in 1972   though clearly
poems are not much like
you   in fact i imagined
yesterday telling a friend
"we can only love
purely and fully

someone quite different
from ourselves"
and i had you in
mind   though i know
the generalization like
most to be untrue

in my poetry class
i am teaching george oppen
a poet of the greatest
integrity one still interested
in truth   he would i know
encourage me (& perhaps has
in writing this poem) to
test poetry in the face
of the worst events

if the words have value
they have value there too

so we come to a place
of dwindling conversation
of friends calling and crying
with you   of walkers
and wheelchairs and
hospice   of your softening
voice your constricted
throat
          a long putt
dying at the hole
the ball does turn &
drop but believe me
it's no occasion for joy

we've played
we play
it's a shot
we've got to hit

loss installs itself
among us beckons

ever lapsing
light

12/6/95

here we are
together again
as desired
let us say yes
to where we
find ourselves
& to what
must happen
let us say
yes to the time
we do have
as it is given
to us to dwell
there equably
& i will witness
with you going
as i can
knowing this
as privilege
awe &

awful
the opening you
are entering

not one prinCipally given to words
but works Hard these
lAst days
to wRite a series of thank you notes
the one to warren worries him a Lot
hE can't get it right
with the noSe

bLeeds the
trAnsfusions and the other
interruptions
not exactly a craZy last task but an
odd choicE for he has been
typically a moRe quiet though heartfelt
correspondent

∼

this is his wrong though givEn name the way
fanya Spelled it
legally hiS but never what i
heArd him called

~

        he seleCted
            cHarles after his father's "chaim"
and then as he told it with a shrUg the guys
               Called him
          chucK

~

grace & concentration in
athletics exactness no
bullshitting & he wouldn't
taught & expected
practice & rapt
attention that
there is
the prospect of
getting it right
which he
on occasion
did

hard to believe
for example
at Pasatiempo
(both witnessed)
a week apart
on the same hole
made double eagle

& at the end of his life
submitted gladly to

by his standards playing
badly the game the playing
the companionship the beauty
of the place superior
to individual accomplishment

by my uncle stan's conjecture chuck woulD rather go off
                              awaY from us not be a
                                        bother an
                    off rhyme wIth the
                              Native american
                                   custom the old one ill
                    wanderinG off to die alone

        does he know he won't make it to hawaii
        or does he express the wish to go there for our
        benefit to give us and him some hope for his strength
        some modest reprieve an unexpected few extra
        days he says he would go knowing he would not
        come back   he says there he could count on
        being warm   being in the sun   is this
        the simple boy from san jose taking with his wife
        one last glorious vacation   or some unconscious
        desire to be like the hawaiians   a ceremony
        he has seen   the outrigger canoes paddling
        away from diamond head   orchid petals
        scattered on the sea   and finally his ashes
        scattered too   these questions are *my*
        conjectures   he has expressed his wishes simply
        with no intention   i suppose   of being enigmatic

12/8/95

against death upon
mom's desk i see
the several
books : *perfect*
health & love,
medicine, & miracles

today i will
price out rates
for cremation
in the grim
humor we share
you say
"son, get me
a good deal"

and i will
since the acute
& confusing grief
is for now
a way's away

when you told me you wanted cremation you told me about your
conversation with dr. pearlstein as he neared death. he too chose
cremation, but he so hated the predatory mortuary business that
he researched california law, the pertinent specification : "must be
cremated in a suitable container." those last two words gave the
funeral homes their opening – "wouldn't you want your loved one
etc." dr. pearlstein specified in his will that he wished to be cre-
mated, and that in keeping with california law, he wished to be
cremated in "a suitable container." which he specified as a large
brown paper bag.

12/11/95 – return – airplane

crying has tired my eyes

being distant above the earth is fine

being high up & going against the erasing clouds
is fine

the anger at the arrangements that didn't work out
can be seen now as a desirable acting out

specifically which items will be given away
can be taken care of later

organ donation probably won't work out
since he has a blood disease

they might take his eyes

simple cremation will be easier to arrange
than expected   donna at the mortuary
did not try to sell me lots of extras
we can use our own urn
we can scatter the ashes
whenever we wish
a simple fibreboard box
may house the body
the cremation will be done locally
there will be no mileage charge
for pick up

it is best to gather the obituary information
ahead of time

there are many papers to fill out
there are various benefits to consider
veterans social security and the like

he said definitely "no formal service
& none of that rabbi crap"

people could come back
to the house to eat & talk
that would be ok

lucidity humor no acute pain
a strange way to be dying

       ~

though we may think so
we are not special
unique yes   but not special

       ~

it is just
dying

& it requires
great cooperation

amidst the crying
you learn
a certain singing

       ~

the flowering of a particular
tenderness in his voice
calling out "henry"
and then as i sit
on the bed beside him
that new voice
asking about donating his organs
or giving his saws and miter box
to someone who might need them
a gentle assertive voice
expressive
quite peaceful
really

12/22/95

ever exacting
light

it cannot be told
not his life not
the dying not a single
day cannot be
told properly cannot be
told fully not
possible to account for
the fine gradations
of change the in
explicable shiftings
from weaker to stronger
& back again not
possible to be exactly
faithful to any

instance the nose
begins to bleed &
then it stops
zeno's arrow is
always in trans
it & every breath
is the same as
a last breath
which we who
love him listen
for and listen
toward trying to
distinguish one
from another when
a true telling
would enter into
the precisely in
distinct the anon
ymously individual
gray gradations
of the arrow's
consequential
but unknowable
flight
we talk instead
of smoked salmon
a dill potato bread
jane found at
vincent's a roasted
new potato salad
the hungers
of an instant

choy ling calls
unaware of how

sick you are
not knowing you
cannot go to hawaii
that you won't make
her new year's party
she among the living
& crying with you on the phone
through the sobbing you do
tell her to give to charity
all you have stored over there

mom yesterday was certain
you were dying certain
it would be soon
too weak to sit up
too weak to turn over in bed
two hours later
you called me
feeling better
and we talked about
food and football
moving as we all seem to
from certainty to certainty
none encompassing
all that much
never quite on the mark

~

knowing this   to partial

to be   departures

the arrow   going

of my ways   going slowly

partial   by degrees

∽

12/27/95

judicious
use

his vanishing
voice

says only
i

am very
tired

∽

the i itself is tired out, gives way to the generic human, foetal,
painfully dependent, unable to move on its own, the steady
weight loss, distended belly, teeth no longer fit right scrape
and bruise the gums, food loses its appeal, the voice grows
softer, a pitiful whisper, still articulate, still lucid, amidst the
terrible embarrassment of every act requiring help, how else
to sit up, or shave, or urinate, how else to bathe, or eat, or
shit, inside the battle between acceptance and anger, resig-
nation and self-pity, as ever his specific behavior (the i
that does survive) placid, equable, humorous, nonetheless
in the context of more encompassing sleep

~

suffused
in light

~

12/29/95

once again an
experimental
drug : *leukine*
just approved
& you begin the
shots   that
& another drug

for your mouth
some way to
break the pain
to change the
starvation diet
gums too sore
to slobber through
matzo ball soup
flown up from LA

sammy your nurse
suspects the gum
sores may be a
sign of thrush

an odd name
when you think
about it for a

disease of mouth
& throat a
fairly common fungus
in infants

did Frost
in his
pastoral exactness
have this in
mind when he
wrote "thrush
music – hark!"
a harking up
a constricted
music strangling
the rush
the babe placed
among the bul-
rushes floats toward
or sticks in the
throat of
some dumb destiny

"Far in the pillared dark
Thrush music went –

Almost like a call to come in
To the dark and lament"

Frost answered back
"I would not come in"
& gave his numerous
specific refusals
so much was he
secretly in love

with grief
and the vigor
of his own resistance

and you have said
equally clearly
you will come in:

if these two
medicines do not
work you have
told dr. rubin
to leave you alone

this
i understand

~

1/3/96

and for a time
the new drugs
seem to work

one morning
the sores
all of them
fall out of
your mouth

& you begin to
walk again
you go out
you visit

[46]

mom sells the
business

the mystical *chi*
for a time is restored

i savor each
phone call
the daily confirmation
of your renewed
voice your will
under these conditions
to live

oddly
at the hospital
the blood numbers
red white platelet
show no
significant change

∽

1/5/96

is the poem co
incident with
your own stepping
over
          what
reasonably of the two
can be fused

if you as yesterday
get to the restaurant

& find you cannot
get out of the car
& that mom must
therefore take you home
under such conditions
what is it that the poem
is obligated to do

professions of love
seem perfunctory
though i know too
the best elegies
are early & often

when the love has been
clearly if not inventively
stated   the poem
then does what it
always does
among other things
mark time

～

1/6/96

of sudden
of a sudden

of books
the sudden love
so these
could be the one
tee-tum

a dumb surprise
among
the panoply of singings

your rhythm
dad
of absolute
interest
day to day
hour to hour

if i call you
every day
if i call you
every hour
i can get down to
an increment of time
in which change
cannot take place

that anti
epiphanic space
the im
perceptible
modulation
of current circumstance

not repetition
but as stein
had it
minute
differences in
insistence

and somehow
everyone comes to be
an old one

and when we
look closely
very closely

"it is a very
difficult thing
to know anything
of the being
in any one"

~

1/9/96

terri said maybe you *are*
after all in this reprieve
getting to have
some of an "old age"
crotchety   focused
talking about this
sonofabitch
& telling the handyman
who's late again
and unprepared
he's full of shit
worried too about
your teeth their fit
their slippage on your gums
and goddamned if anyone's
going to pester you into

eating when you've decided
you won't   hurray i say
for all your asinine
stubbornness the vigor
of your resistance an
imperfect pain in the ass
a role til now
you had been forgetful of

&

a poem a cell
the structures of activity
motion coincident with
a complex equation
as you move

through space & time

&

a
precise nature
of dying
is that it doesn't
seem
to be going
on

and
because that *is*
the case
we honestly
don't much

turn our attention
to
it

~

words
the similar
ciphers

the poem
determined
by the length
of your life

i don't know
for you
whether it's comforting
or upsetting
to know there are
memorials such as this
being built for you

a pyre
a crypt
similar ciphers

pixel
of light
released
beneath the letters

~

1/12/96

as had been proud
not the least of which
the supple single words

i have in this intended
& asking of you as you
the exact metric   made of blanks

you'd love to see   (& i would too)
the Packers kick the shit out of the Cowboys

"except walking expressly"   *cell / lyn hejinian / 20*

saxophone
his blowing adequate to being
blew it no simpler than it is
exactly scratchy   her voice
very melodic

so obviously not

consecutive
accumulating
somehow nonetheless

      ～

1/13/96

so long as i am
reading this particular
book   of final
conversations with

john cage   you will
                              no need to
complete the equation

in this the miraculous
the stretched temporary
of adequate duration
lose gratitude
return to more normative
structures of diffuse
attention

you not central to every
thought you not the boss
of tragic narrative

words again go out to play
sniff other shrubs
seep morph shift stutter
heuristic twist
"thought's torsion"
in the instant
of its thinking

healthy
or moreso
as each
injected with
the experimental
which in this
instance
opens up
time
& some of it
together

[54]

leukemia
to lupine
the beautiful
pea pod

∾

1/14/96

    rough
    as a cob

    difficult
    as herding cats

    so as you go
    you are changing
    your thinking in
    relation to it

told me in detail about garzone's
bad investment   not everyone wants
a contemporary look & at 895
who wants to share a drive
way   & radiant heat scares
people

    we don't know
    if our own experiences
    are especially typical
    i enjoy your company
    and our conversations

    i have no idea
    whether it's that way

for most sons
i hope with my own
son we will talk
to each other with
mutual interest well
into my old age
work to imagine

≈

1/18/96

speaking
relatively
a spell
of approximate
health
& utterly
improbable

≈

1/27/96

& so pre
sent a present
of

trips to costco
orchard supply
trader joe's
an evening conducting
the annual homeowners'
meeting   each day

[56]

some major outing
a lunch   a trip
to the office
then you stood up
took a shower
shampooed your hair
dressed yourself
barely needing the walker

you've driven the new
car once or twice
went then at mom's
insistence to show
your doctor what was
happening
shocked him
into a thorough exam
the white count doubled
the platelets doubled
no one talks of
recovery or exactly
what this miracle
is or isn't
a reprieve an
unexpected return
of strength

as with most
other living
unforeseen

1/28/96

for carrying
or calibrating

test results yield
specific momentary data

vs. your
subjective impression

the two generally
in parallel

extremely precise &
thus precisely enigmatic

telling jokes again
slowly   & drawn out
"henry   there were these three doctors
who died & went before St. Peter
to find out if they would get into heaven
the first doctor said, 'i devoted my life to cancer research;
i made some small discoveries   i tried my best.'
st. peter said, 'ok   you get to go to heaven'
the second doctor said, 'all my life i served the poor
i never made much money   i saved the ones i could'
st. peter said, 'ok   you get to go to heaven'
the third doctor said, 'i developed four of the largest
HMOs in the region'   st. peter thought
then said, 'for you   i've got some good news
& some bad news   the good news is   you get to go to heaven
the bad new is   you can only stay three days'"

a return to banality
nothing particularly evil there

no intensifying difference
back to the oblique   the deflected *a re*
turn or retreat into ungraspable dailiness

1/31/96

consecutively
the succession
of his thoughts
become projects
some of which
he must get
done stubborn
is another way
to put it
& like his mother
what he's stubborn
about
will not
get talked out
the garage his clothes the files
a set of metonyms
at what duration
does time become
significant
cherished in short
spans
at some length & beyond
inevitably banal

he does much more
thinking
i know it

     ~

2/3/96

i have the luxury of waiting
& you have the refusal to eat most foods
& mom may begin to sell the place in honolulu
& slowly you are
cleaning & rearranging the garage
moving as we do
unnoticed
through our variable temporal relations
yours (& thus ours, in part)
from cherish to grateful
to the more familiar tub
of routine daily bathing
from time felt & pondered
now returned
in what we call
reprieve or
miracle
restored to the illusion
of endlessness
the merciful indistinctness
of its
(actually our)
disappearance

rather than your
daily worsening
the markers become again

sporting events & the weather
Magic's return
as a power forward
Phil Mickelson's seven straight one-putts
to win the tournament
your sunshine & our winter storm

here sporadic snow flakes
a few birds rummage
among the sharp holly bushes
the iced over roads
(blank paper-like
with a few semi-
visible habitual tracks)
stop us

2/16/96
Dallas to San Jose

of love
the decisive one

again flying west
this time with some
finality

after his extended reprieve
a disappearance of
the expressively heroic
the miraculous last
burst of doing
the atypical heart
felt conversations

these last two weeks
principally foetal
the generic sleeping
little ability or desire
to eat or drink

then peeing the bed
a bad fall &
his body pinned
between the wall
& the toilet

a day in the hospital
more transfusions
but no change
in energy level
conversation
a whisper in which
he claims to be
in no pain claims
to be comfortable

dr. rubin
determines you
won't leave the hospital
that the leukemic cells
have taken over

anyone's touch
is painful to you

you have promised
to hang on
until i arrive

these narrative
arrangements
are not ours
to make

if you die
before i arrive
that is fine
especially if it
is a good
& easy death

as for my wishes
i would gladly
sit with you
the sporadic whispered
conversations a
holding of your hand
the unfocused
opening of your eyes

love calls us
or so i feel
to the whole cycle
of a loved one's
life the dying too
is holy that time
together sacramental
instructive
intimate
enigmatic

when i spoke with you
yesterday on the phone
your humor remained

intact   after a long
pause   you asked
still mocking your
mother & the recurrent
question of her
senility in her 95th year
"so how's bigshot?"
and i told you
what alan, now
seven, was doing
that afternoon

i didn't tell you
that he prayed
for you & that he
asks with tenderness
and abstract curiosity
about what the leukemia
is   and what it's
doing to you

oddly
on the way to his
school two
days ago we
heard radio news
of a promising
canadian treatment
for leukemia

~

for many years
i have been
blessed & protected

[64]

by the outposts
of four grandparents
they are gone now
and you will die
& i
will cease to be
a son

more mornings
come
a few times
every day

of
the dying
the living
die
into

it matters:
your night nurse
is jewish
she's been she says
much among
the dying
& you she says
are not quite
there yet
& will make it
til i get there
& maybe
a day or so
beyond

as then
the final man

we age into
a caricature
of our pre
decessors

2/29/96

to yearn
in the direction
one is

to do so
fully

without reservation
he
seemed to
do so
&
died

having moved
to an interior

for a time
he had
the capacity
to whisper

to raise
his right hand

[66]

sometimes to grasp
one of ours

sometimes to lay it

on his own chest
& moan

closed eyes
shallow breathing

a shot
of morphine

an hour
or so
later

the eyes
rolled back

& that
was
that

call it
peace
or
an end

from
which

a million
narratives
depart

a flow
of emotion

as best i
know by
the term
kensho

that kind of
flash
which
changes a life
(mine i
know)

thereafter
each new
instance
of human
consolation

simultaneously
heals
&
tears open

∾

Wendy had given you permission to quit struggling, to "go be with god." Odd, I thought, she's never once I can recollect ever said anything about god.

Earlier, she had thrown herself on you sobbing, "he never did anything mean to anyone in his life." I said, "oh yes he did. The first golf club he gave me, when I was five, was a one iron." And you, already losing speech, had not, two hours from death, lost your sense of humor, and you chuckled and gave a faint smile.

You rallied just enough to acknowledge mom's presence, my presence, Terri's, and Stan and Linda's. But you were fully into yourself, or somewhere else.   You are gone. We go on.

3/6/96

there is a

    O
  R C
   K

in the stream
around which
the water flows

if not
the physical body
what are we

that pantheon

maybe that is

the classic book

written & barely

noticed larry

snuck it by

it comes back at us

yes john trust

above all others

the dead their

conversation

in which you

take part dip

as k b said

an oar in

the water

& help

the others paddle

The Abacos

It is a call to fluency.

Driving on the left

can be a tourist attraction

since a modest but

noticeable difference is,

after all, a commodity

of considerable interest to us.

Misestimation becomes clear

in bold relief but only

retrospectively. It's each

to his own electronic

communication device, a

planetary membrane of inter-

connected momentary importance.

As Henry wrote by hand

beside the pond, "and

what if when the telegraph

line is connected, etc."

Early morning laps are

best. John seems able

to write with great enthusiasm

from the same perspective

again and again. Is once

not enough, though once,

we know, is no career.

Here, the conch meat

must be beaten and

battered to be made

adequately tender. John

makes it possible to say

almost anything and feel

the act to have importance,

a *fin de siècle* project in

equipoise, postcolonial tone, &

a worldly perhaps universal

lamentation, not over historical

forces nor the politically

predatory, but for one's own

quotient of intermittently dismaying

gradual decay. If you continue

to pedal you will be propelled

forward, patches of loose gravel

not withstanding. In fact, John

seems always on vacation,

as if perpetually bemused

with no fiduciary

or occupational concern.

But what, you say, of

an appropriate *literary* tone?

The dead are still

among us as we recall

and say their favorite

phrases. Here, the currency

exchanges one for one. I

bother my son

to eat his supper as my father

pestered me. "The house

is a mango vinaigrette."

The intense orange blossoms

of the flame tree perfectly

expressed the longing in

Clarissa's heart. Did I

write that or did I read it

in the hardbound book

held by the woman in

the lounge chair beside me,

red enameled nails, a crisp

white visor, long blonde hair

drawn in a ponytail,

long hair for women again the fashion

though there's no discussion

of its meaning. Everything

changes but the will to change.

The hammock criss-crosses

your back. Tan cautiously.

As vacations go, it's a good

value, transfers not included.

No one expects to be

brought up short, to be,

as it were, short-changed,

at least not before one

delightful appearance, perhaps

among the palms, perhaps

among the ever present

casuarina pines, of the

indigenous and colorful abaco parrot.

Your son, I think,

will be the first to spy one.

Nevertheless, the marvels are

marvelous, moments of rapt

attention within the purple fan

& elkhorn coral, the barrier reef

of Guana Cay. The ferry man

quit school at fourteen, and

took over his father's job.

On Guana Cay two teachers

split the fifteen students

& each teach grades one

through six.

And when your nine year old

son pops his head up from

snorkeling in the barrier reef,

having seen the neon blue

dotted fish, proclaims he will

remember this day the rest

of his life, you know the vow

is not within his power, that you

at unwise expense have chosen

this vacation as charged antidote

to time's power, glad your

family unit has survived

the chazerye & more serious

turbulence of this particular year.

Each spinning sentence perhaps

John too would admit constitutes

a class of evasion, a literary

privilege stemming from a caste

of study, a tonal castanet that

clicks or whisks one away from

the grander corridors of economic

constriction. So too with the inward

turning of family romance or

its sibling ecosystem, personal

rumination. Nonetheless, the sun

sets, and Rudy the black lab

comes back with a small bird

held loosely in his mouth.

Yes, she says, the market

has a jar of spanish olives!

The Pegasus pulls into

 the yacht harbor. Fritz,

on his day off, rides the ferry

over to Guana Cay and back.

The bass of the reggae tune

reverberates from the poolside bar.

Vacations are for decision-making,

Hope Town by ferry (shlepping the snorkel

gear) or Treasure Cay by car,

a replay of protracted

familial closeness: who

gets to do what when. We pay

for an irritating ease and prospect

for sporadic marvels, the school

of blue-striped fish beside the elkhorn coral,

seventy and eighty clear feet beneath us.

Mornings warm as home

but foreign. Your son loves

the pennies with the stars on them

still utterly immune from an adult

sense of money, though he sits up

late at night reading his game

book *Quest*, rolling the dice, and asking

the meaning of words like rune,

pompous, sentry, escort, and trident.

His fiction too includes money

and the prospect of victorious sequence.

Reading John's poems is a vacation

tinged in various exotic packages and plans;

each exacts a price, is never particularly

mean-spirited, in fact, is quite congenial,

soothing, amusing, you'll *want* to come back

having noticed the off-rhyme with

your specific dailiness, John

having made an extensive new

hammock of great comfort this late

afternoon. Look. Palm trees above

fan and whisper in the soothing

breeze, and one of those large

black birds with sharp wings

and trailing legs glides east or west,

and you nod off having achieved

a complex resolution next to impossible

at home.

       The truly wealthy have

their own island, or share among

themselves a private residential one.

The name is Scotland Cay, and the

harbour is clearly marked: for owners

only, and their guests.

Today,

once again, I am John's guest

(having purchased an examination

copy which ostensibly cost me

only for shipping and handling).

Actually it is our soul we see

in sudden flashes of clear colorful

coral and feel simple lucid gratitude

for being alive. These insights

come at a price and dwell far

away from the suicidal ideations

that pock-marked the previous year.

We come here to get away,

and, equally, to be *here*.

The ferry to Hope Town or

the car to Little Harbour.

Places known to be "cute" don't

interest you, and so begins

the difficulty (and the pleasure)

of your perspective, for

yours, and here is part of your

affinity with John, is *not* an aesthetic

opposed to beauty.

                    Typically,

miracles prove inexplicable. Yes,

our beach has no seaweed

because a young man carts it away

each dawn. It may take him an hour

or two. So too with the appearance

of the fresh blue towels.

As with everything, from breakfast to

death, even if we have called all

the pronouns into contemporary question,

"we do it all for you." Our room
is next to housekeeping, noisy, yes,

but adequate proximity to overhear

the contours of a percussive language

not addressed to us.

To make of leisure an occupation,

even that option invokes a smiling

double, leisure the territory you

occupy, John, until it's assumed

to belong to you, (I knew

you were the true

owner of Scotland Cay).

From one side of the native coin,

your bemused face squints out

of the half-opened cabana door.

Everyone adores the one who seems

to know, who reassures so knowingly,

and with memorable loquaciousness,

tells how there are no difficult ideas we need

to latch onto, only learn and re-learn

laconic attention to this peachy keen

sensation, a mixed drink three parts stasis

one part gradual change, sip it

and listen to the similar clicking

of palm fronds in pleasant

morning breeze. Memorable

as a barrette left beside the swimming pool.

Fuck. It's Sunday, and the Christian

bacterial infection rages, and no doubt

someone will berate me about Jesus.

Goddamn. Let a hundred jumpers jump,

but please leave me the fuck alone

to worship as I see fit. Call the golf course

my church, and I don't mean that

to be funny. God knows I get

enough text-based stuff the rest of

the time. (I am Jewish,

therefore some country clubs still

forbid me.) Hang on a minute

& I'll give you what you want,

a breeze, or cloud cover, a different

vista, a piece of wisdom, or the kind

of ironizing that makes your alienation

feel worth it all. Say, a comic

frame of acceptance. Skip the Jesus

crap, anyone tell me where I can

see one of those colorful abaco parrots?

Instead, the ubiquitous mockingbird

bobs on the railing. And I rail back,

"we in America want something singular."

Cha-ching, cha-ching,   of thee I sing.

In Hope Town the three of us

snorkel among caverns of coral,

hundreds of different fish, blue,

yellow, black, several barracuda,

numerous large grouper. My last

time out, edging along the reef

fighting my way out as the tide

comes in, I look down in forty

or fifty feet of water and see

below a school of fish a reef shark

nearly my own size looking back

up at me. Fear quickens such

memorable instants—a jolt or

tonic exact as the poem's reputed

lyrical sublime. Silver glint

and mutually focused eyes.

Ghoul, ajar, stimuli, undead

mark the wave of questions

from my son's vacation reading.

Go ahead, son, inevitably you've

got it right: hang onto the vampire

stories and a small collection

of Bahamian coins, the variegated dime

with two leaping fish,

the shiny penny with a singular star.

At some point in time, you,

as I, will grow weary (and perhaps

worshipful) of the enchanter emeritus,

find the charms a little goofy,

the remembered moments a bit too neatly

retrofitted, and may substitute a slightly

roughened set of your own, more about

your own frustrated tugging against an

invisible leash of compliance and proximity,

glimmerings of which we see beneath

this purchased time of imagined release.

Work Ups

each of us is moving away from
    something and moving
    toward something else

each of us of many ages in this
    age at this moment is
    writing away from
    something and perhaps
    writing into something else

any iteration of what that prior
    something is   produces
    controversy

so too does any iteration of
    what that something else is

or how to move away from and
    for what reasons

of many ages   each of us
    away from

to some of us the newness no
    longer seems new

in transition   in transit
    a turning preoccupied with
    capacities of the genre

some in this age are busy
    circling back

there is a buzz among us where
    we came from

. . . it has been a familiar
syndrome in American poetry
to deny the poetic efficacy of
collective action; to insist on
the integrity of the heroic
ego; and to mistrust anything
that smacks of the committee
room. These have been
disabling denials because
they set impossible demands
on the individual, as well as
discounting the facticity of
social reality. (Jed Rasula)

"Our poets" is deceptively
democratic; in fact, such a
phrase has never implied a
radius bigger than an exclu-
sive country club, and we
can't discount the snobbism
of "good form" that attends
canonical choices in such an
environment. (Jed Rasula)

Every order of poetry finds
itself, defines itself, in strife
with other orders. A new
order is a contention in the
heart of existing orders.
(Robert Duncan)

. . . each idea of poetry in so
far as it is vitally concerned is
charged with a conviction
that it has a mission to

there is something ludicrous
in saying it this way

of course it always involves
history which is why the
word *field* is pastoral and
electric

after shagging flies in the
outfield we each count on
a turn at the plate

change, to recreate the heart
of poetry itself. Each of us
must be at strife with our own
conviction on behalf of the
multiplicity of convictions at
work in poetry in order to give
ourselves over to the art, to
come into the idea of what
the world of worlds or the
order of orders might be.
(Robert Duncan)

This One

said among the many ways   & went about it

    looked out   & saw how it was

      felt it close by   a moth sliding up the window

    felt it at a distance   & then for months not at all

carried   not by the seeing   not by the hearing

    carried   by the intimation

      ～

of our own gestures

          plot or meaning

              you've got to be
             kidding me

         ～

child face down   kicking & screaming

    deep in the night

      sang a lullaby   over the crying child

     sang what assurances she could muster

wise songs   in russian   in yiddish

my childhood spent in the presence

of melodious   & unintelligible

languages

you could trust the sound

the laughter   the mischief

the look in sonia's eyes

~

standing on green linoleum   a single red teapot

in the middle of their kitchen

forty-three years ago   and again

that sink   cupboards

stove   return

& my grandparents' own   distracted pleasure

~

to each is given

one two or three places to see

to live & know

(such as knowing goes)

a local sense

as buddhist maxim has it

any set of particulars

more than adequate

∼

these people conquered nothing

but had a stretch   of graceful living

moving from new york to california
to take part in western promise

to whisper   assimilation

small shop keepers   marveling

in quiet defeat

at the onslaught

of mall   & supermarket

their humor   opened moments

～

certain said the weak among

set the wheat among

said defeat among

to feed among

～

as the dead return   we listen to them

have them   & keep them   in mind

in the surprising ways   that they remain

memorable

ways that pry us

apart

the stars

       & the distance

             between them

    ≈

if what i say

       is not impossible

    why bother

   we will be there   soon enough

        ≈

serendipitous   encryption

code cracker   enraptured

"breaker breaker
          cable to the ace"

"which channel you on?"

"o live!" said the olive

"for give" said the guava

"my dictionary
               or yours?"
                              said the gunslinger

no need to personalize any of this

allow plenty of time
                              for your gift to arrive

"breaker   breaker
                              cable to the ace"

∾

this particular not knowing

                              is not a problem

not knowing   for sure   whether i am

an atheist   an agnostic   a believer

whatever i would say or sing   this particular instant

must also admit   *here* is the door

that ten minutes later

or a week   or a year from now

all bets are off

that *movement*

    is   the living of it

        & that which might be

must also   periodically   turn toward

    & away

        ∼

the atoms drip

        the atoms cripple

there   in mirror image

    our brothers & sisters in the craft

    write about their personal

    feelings

the atoms drip

        the atoms cripple

the devices make possible

    oh   the places
    you'll go

[97]

at the fundamental

you don't know

on the ice

warm   lightweight   traction

the atoms drip

the atoms cripple

∾

of virtuous love   & sadly state

the love of poetry

disrupts all other love

∾

i do not think i   will find that home

as a thinker   or as a poet

some *do* find it

have it made   for them

most   do not

& thus live

[98]

in some astonishment
                    doing what we do
                                    having
        some erratic   but recurring sense
                                    of its potential import
& have then   no home   for what we do

        find it instead

            in enduring conversation

    with the yet to be

        & with the already dead

given over

        by language

            to language

    water   passes through our hands

    air   circulates throughout the biosphere

        & in our lungs   & blood   & syllables

        converting   & combining

        ever   & again

i do not think i   will find that home

as a thinker   or as a poet

                        some do *find it*

have it made   for them

                ∿

        "hello   m' night
                        illuminate . . . "

so you know

                any two similar sounds

                        do not warrant my attention

        witness wear
                        a local christian clothing company
                is laying off employees

                        there is   however
                        a christian ballet company
                        coming to town

        gotta love the maccabees

                        who hit quickly   as a hammer

        "hello   m' night
                        illuminate . . . "

                ∿

he makes mischief   this one

    makes the prank   the slang   the off-song   lets slip

    the fuck-word   among the kids at the family gathering

he makes mischief   this one   affirms

    play   & convulsive laughter   that wreck

    & deepen   all sober observations   all political
    insistence

    the psychoanalytical   being argued around him

undercuts their temples & their churches

    all the while   early mornings   reading

        his own sacred texts   a mist
            of fog   & edifying discomfort

        party to the inexplicable   & the coincidental

                he makes mischief   this one

                          ∼

then   maybe this would be it

                              or   then again

set passage   set sail   among a simple

            group of words

      the specific grit

                  of each

                        not translatable

spoken by one   in one circumstance

                              one middle aged
            man   after listening to the tornado story
                  he looks a little stupefied   is quiet for
            a second or two

                  and then he sighs
            & says a single drawn out syllable: *dog*

            with specific regional inflection   & the full force
                  of the oddly twisted path
                              of his own life

      each utterance
                  potentially
                              saturated
            with its own   otherness

maybe   this would be it

     among a simple   group of words

       to savor
          the specific grit   of each

   the sponge   *the simplest of them*

Diamond Head

6/3/99

my place & the dimmer
switch
        low tide &
a boy browses
coral formations
too young too young
am i for grandiloquent
retrospection to say
what i have strived for
& thus to gain your
sweet assent
              dawn
plus an hour Diamond
Head clouds trade breeze
coffee Oppen   Rod's new
Protective Immediacy early
birds warble & shift
about   words test
the water weather
day erasures re
visions quips & sudden
recollections whose
goddamn watch beeps every
hour
      not the woman my
mother with the skin
graft a smooth
strip from the back
of her ear
placed gently below
her right eye this
doctor she says "an *artist*
his friends are all writers

and painters" she
says he's something
very special   & i
see her calling out to
her mother & father long
dead still trying to
claim their attention
to convince them of
something   show them
once & for all
that she has earned
their approval   & we
the living family love her
even as we tire of
her perpetual exaggerations

praise be to our mother
of exaggerated claims

~

dawn somehow a place
outside erratic cacophonous
happenings that clarity
George avers from which
nothing myself i can
think of & love each

~

she may sleep on
somehow oblivious to
light birds palms
coffee surf first
workers tidying tables

~

here at the outer
reach of Austronesian
settlement   from dugout
canoe to balanced out
rigger   a modification
of considerable consequence
from China to Taiwan to
Indonesia Polynesia &
Hawai`i by 500 A.D.

~

Keo's has moved &
the portions seem smaller
crispy duck in plum sauce
& cilantro   spring rolls
wrapped in Manoa lettuce
please us & the evil
jungle prince burns our lips
jet lag grabs the youngest one
& he grimaces &
nods off at the table
while we clean our plates

~

smooth kona coffee
brain food of
early morning

~

what goes with what
& how   & why

anything can
& has   & will

said i meant to
choose among those
options

at this time quiet
exactness of each thing
has a chance

then dragged into
the equally true
amalgamation

≈

George:

I might at the top of my ability stand at a window
and say, look out; out there is the world.   CP | 186 | Route

that window
i think
had for a long time
been the site of poetry
and now i am certain
it is not

though i drag my ability still
to some prospect   point & sound
(i live in the aftermath
of that romantic infection)

if a city upon a hill
then necessarily *not* a beacon
but a teeming site multiply
shining in complex artificial light
product of our wires and generators
going on and off

6/4/99

having will acquire
and leaves detectable
traces   food germs
weapons particular language
terms necessitated

now the chef
makes mention of cilantro
balsamic wasabi arugula
couscous & risotto a rim
of chatter & ingestions soft
ware mappings swift
succession of pleasing dis
tractions a trajectory
of specialization &
redistribution over which
we converse
                poetry too
proffers new dishes
serves up a succulent

lyric with hint
of imported documen
tation feeding what need ex
tending an allegedly
fundamental investigation
an inquiry into
how we pass our time

        ∼

when serve evades
& afterwards when
given specific coordinates

6/5/99

in the newly imagined
children's book Prince
Pudgeator-the-Chicken-Hearted
lacks all aggression &
as cat gallops with a
singularly humorous caterpillar-
like gait   he is afraid
of everything has a blank
serious expression & is
utterly loveable

            plan the day
by traffic patterns & what
others are doing
            your
other life five hours ahead
inhabited by reliable housesitters

~

Senator Stentorian his affable
smile & cocksure noncommittals
raise among some of us a general
suspicion about any sort
of I-say pronouncement

so that George this morning
sounds romantic & heroic
in a naïve sort of way:

of which I chose the harbor
and the sea   CP | 127 | Monument

how then to say what
needs saying to wrestle
with the particularly telling
confusions of the time
& do so in a way free
of excessive pandering free
of a corrupt & entangling
tradition of reader-manipulation

the fragmentary the steadily
disturbed *has* that moral high
ground but also a stylized
aridity & its own disabilities

sing then the sentence &
its constituent elements?

friends & the mechanisms
of friendship
            quotidian efforts

toward the heroic
                    is the dry
ice ready to go into the chest?

         ∾

merely decorous rumination
moves few to action or
amusement
                    i sing   i sing
of icing on the cake

6/6/99

the committee convenes monthly
to hear from the various
subcommittees & to go over
what other members of the committee
already know   at the end
of the year the committee
will issue its final report

         ∾

for George the guilt
of privilege is never
far away
            my father
sold shoes & children's
toys, liquor, & finally
real estate   over time
a shopkeeper of increasing
abstraction
            and so

for his son from the class
room to the administrator's
desk
      for George the repairing
gesture returns attention
to fundamentals

The astronomic light
That wakes a people
In the painful dawn   *CP | 114*

or to
          watch
At the roots
Of the grass the creating
Now   *that tremendous*
plunge
       calling as he does
nonetheless to that *father*
Of fatherhood
Who haunts me   *CP | 126*

the waves this early morning
are one to three and adequate
by 7 a.m. to uphold surfers
and kayakers who ride &
surmount the waves in a
seemingly not so painful dawn

the exactness they practice
is fundamental
         & perhaps
as their fathers wished

well above them tourists

look out from the platform
of the dormant crater

joggers & bicyclists circle
the park & in the invisible
interior rapid hands prepare
an enormous breakfast buffet

ironic witness may be an avail
able pose
one graceful
& accepted way down the
slope of the wave
but in the long run of
little consequence
                    better
thirty or so years of
restraint than a
less than essential
poetic chatter

what then to say
that matters now

i must have this first hour
of the day before the others
wake into our conversing

& i ask that you consider
what gets said in this hour
& ask as well that we consider
what George might have called

an adequate ethics one
that connects that early

hour to our conduct
the rest of this & every day

say it knowing you may
think as i have fuck
plainspoken poetic speech
& its weary manipulations

flawed rhetoric or not
the particular questions
remain at hand

& the fathers &
the mothers of them

6/8/99

"our next contestant,
Porcini Polenta, hails
from the island of Oahu, Bob . . . "

"true or false: when the first settlers
arrived they infected the natives
by means of their credit cards . . . "

ten thousand years from now
we are told there will be
another Hawaiian island

where i sit sunny & dry
seven miles inland
170 inches annual rainfall

the trail we took to

Manoa Falls supposedly
one thousand years old

the banyan tree displaces
& uproots what gets
in its way

the young boy with the sketch pad
remains on the hau terrace
while the adults debate what
to do tomorrow   with detailed
black ink precision   he draws
aliens & wrestlers   bosses of
many levels   begins a series about
a chicken-hearted cat named
Prince Pudgeator
                    what does this
child become
                    and in what relation
does he stand to the newly
forming island?
                    or for that
matter   to popular new models
of the palm pilot

        ∼

my absent father & his
enabling humor   he is
here quite presently in every
adventure   in daily chores
& in extended conversations

        ∼

what matters is what persists?
so poetry aspires to be
like the cockroach capable
of surviving an atomic blast?
how can you tell
one Mary Higgins Clark novel
from another?

of topical interest
a topical ointment
the saying of the day

amateurism in defense of
a beloved product is no vice

      ~

for George the horror
of wealth is its
camouflaging cacophony

the noise of wealth   CP | 87 | Guest Room

The clamor of wealth – tree
So often shaken – it is the voice

Of Hell.
              guilty of obscuring
fundamental questions
                   & thus
part of his own persistent struggle
to see clearly   *the thing*   CP | 90
Happening, filling our eyesight
Out to the horizon –

& to think (& to sing) of that
only
    over & against which
the wealthy exert force
Embattled and despairing   CP | 89

Mysteriously George then says
It is the courage of the rich

Who are an avant garde   CP | 90

Near the limits of life –

courageous in what sense?
inevitably so? as they edge
toward an unalterable funda
mental term? George who all his
life was ashamed of his own
modest wealth   acknowledges
as poet his own kinship
with the busy idiocy of
the rich:
          Like theirs   CP | 90

My abilities
Are ridiculous:

—each i suppose based on
desperation   each infected
with a romantic willfulness
inevitably inadequate to the task—

To go perhaps unarmed
And unarmored, to return   CP | 90

Now to the old questions —

6/9/99

in modern times no new
animals have been
domesticated in this respect
our powers of choice
& persuasion are no better
than ten thousand years ago

     ～

is the ocean here
the particular tone
of aqua or turquoise
you came to crave?

     ～

where *do* you want to
go   what *do* you
want to see & who
will want to go there
with you?

     ～

"Rhino-mounted Bantu shock troops   Diamond | 399
could have overthrown the Roman   *Guns, Germs, & Steel*
Empire. It never happened."

[118]

~

a novel would be easier
with plenty of places
for careful description
as long as you can
keep something happening

here
the pace of what happens
is exactly
as it happens

it's raining!

~

a cooler than usual breeze
rattles soothingly across the long
row of plantation shutters
alone in her large bed she stirs
in early morning light
still half asleep she looks up
to the top of Diamond Head
she sees the outlines of figures
of a few people atop the observation
deck   she begins to finger the small
bandage beneath her eye and she recalls . . .

6/11/99

the voices return to me
yes   as voices
& compel their writing

in the dream a relaxed
Jake (in shorts & birkenstocks)
asked me if i would be
ready to play "*string of pearls*" tomorrow

yesterday   scuba diving for
the first time   quite difficult
as in early meditation   to
empty my head of voices
concern with the equipment
attention to the instruction
rather than attention to
the simple present

at Sandy Beach
i place a two-stone
tribute in honor of Chuck
stare up bare volcanic
mountainside to see
clouds go sailing by

say the name of all
say it as a breath

        ∿

some have begun
it is a question then
what we are becoming
my bet is not one thing

would we know it
that primordially trans
formative next step
would we even see it

as with everything
(except birth & death)
the privilege of it
would be   i am
willing to bet
unequally distributed

~

hard from my position here
to get too worked up
in favor of an imagined
indigenous island
when i know the native
peoples came from elsewhere
fifteen hundred years ago
plants trees dogs go back
then to *which* beginnings

what would be an indigenous
poetry when first words &
first language prove to be
tabulation of possessions

sing it then as we are
leaving a complex ethics
of the present a song
of loss & gain the pooling
way of alteration

hot *malasadas* on King
Kamehameha's birthday!

glorious morning
trade breeze caffeine quiet
& a stack of books

easy   too easy   to sink
among our things   to become
their caretaker   anything
but the requisite daily
meditation on death
that great enabler &
true ground of our doing

      ～

when the poetry   ceases to be
about trying to belong

      ～

a hodgepodge   a grab bag
my great Aunt Sonia's
clumsy closet   with a chuckle
when she couldn't figure out
where to put something away
that's where it went
the clumsy closet   eventually
that's what her whole life became
living in a mobile home in
Santa Rosa among stacks of
papers & paintings & carved
figurines   a cigarette in one
hand coffee mug in the other
a piece of toast on the table
confusion fear the bank her
son taking her for a ride

the clumsy closet swirling
all around her until
nothing at all could be put away

~

attend to rectal itch
early in the day

6/12/99

moray   snowflake
slither along the coral
crevice   treasured sightings

subsequent poesis of cuisine
Roy Yamaguchi's masterful
fusion reduction embodied
collages of the locally perfect
this one atop a bed
of purple sweet potato

~

how gluten
imitates meat
edible tarot basket
holds spicy vegetables

the page

~

Fred Wah   when i get home
i look forward to resuming
our conversation

        ∾

sediment settles depending
on tide   awkward
in our flippers   stand still   [adjust downward
so as not to stir up the silt   to eliminate
                                       excess sibilance]

        ∾

this morning George tells me:
I come to know it is home a groping   CP / 252
                                             Confession

down a going
down middle-voice the burgeoning

desolate   magic   the dark
grain

of sand and eternity

how then is this not
a persistent romanticism
the sensitive ego   *is* there
other than the dramatic so
liloquy   eloquent preening
—yes the questions matter—
upon the metaphysician's
favorite rhetorical stage?
must it all come down
to a variegated lament
upon aging & the passage of time

    [124]

6/13/99

the story of desire
having & missing you
scattered with specifics
which make it for another
reader adequately different

& if no heart ever arrives
finally schooled isn't it
reasonable to doubt the value
other than as temporary
amusement & distraction
of this other story too?

～

lyrical essayist sudden
turns & swerves the lip
surf somewhat un
governable music leading
the witness   adequate swell
propels you for an erotic
surge toward the coastline
or back out in it nose
first cutting through
the breaking wave

～

released from the habit
of perpetual metaphorization

～

jumped from the cliff
into the cold deep pool
of Maunawili Falls

~

honor the memory of Chuck
with a large scoop
of corned beef hash

~

Fred Wah's *music*
at the heart of thinking
attunes an appealing pitch

if any persistent tissue bristles pitapat
on the heart's much too excited lip
could be the air's too rare   *Alley Alley | 62 | "one oh five"*
naturally some same body
remembers too late
to search for another wave

~

and of course collision
course proximate collage
of colluding precincts
temple in hearing
sighed into sight

~

George again trumpets
the metaphysical glory
of our labor: *Art*   *CP | 84-85 | From Virgil*
Also is not good

For us
Unless like the fool

Persisting
In his folly

It may rescue us
As only the true

Might rescue us, gathered
In the smallest corners

Of man's triumph.

& if that truth
prove present when
we awaken to any
given instant . . .

to be truthful then
to its infinite con
tingency its perpetual
inconclusiveness
why then trumpet its arrival
at the portal of your
anguished soliloquy
George?
        just
get on with it
man   among

the too many elements

what you articulate
we take as given

~

reading as *chi gong*

writing as *tai chi*

free to quicken the pace

this is your natural life
this is your perfect health

6/14/99

& already we begin
to move away from
where we are

see the place   as falling away from
our momentary   habitation of it

Sunyata Sonata

—for Norman Fischer

1   *(largo – breathing attentively)*

2   *(allegro)*

no ideas
but in things

but things
are not ideas

but *in* things
are ideas?

and aren't
ideas things

where
in things

are ideas

3   *(largo vivace – breathing attentively)*

4   *(allegro)*

in which things
are ideas

in which ideas
are things

no things

but in ideas

know things

but in ideas

the angels
are engines

driving on
driving on

and *in* them?

are ideas?

but in things

no ideas

no ideas

no things

5   *(largo)*

if god stands
outside of death

what can that
know of us

                              star

                              pollen

                                             seed

                                             sky

Lightning Source UK Ltd.
Milton Keynes UK
UKOW04f0152280415

250471UK00002B/57/P